Season to Season

Anita Ganeri

Heinemann
LIBRARY

young
Explorer

www.heinemann.co.uk/library
Visit our website to find out more information about **Heinemann Library** books.

To order:
☎ Phone 44 (0) 1865 888066
🖹 Send a fax to 44 (0) 1865 314091
💻 Visit the Heinemann Bookshop at www.heinemann.co.uk/library to browse our catalogue and order online.

First published in Great Britain by Heinemann Library, Halley Court, Jordan Hill, Oxford OX2 8EJ, part of Harcourt Education. Heinemann is a registered trademark of Harcourt Education Ltd.

Editorial: Jilly Attwood, Kate Bellamy
Design: Jo Hinton-Malivoire
Illustration: Jeff Edwards
Picture research: Kay Altwegg, Ruth Blair
Production: Séverine Ribierre

Originated by Dot Gradations Ltd
Printed and bound in China by South China Printing Company

ISBN 0 431 11405 6 (hardback)
09 08 07 06 05
10 9 8 7 6 5 4 3 2 1

ISBN 0 431 11411 0 (paperback)
10 09 08 07 06
10 9 8 7 6 5 4 3 2 1

British Library Cataloguing in Publication Data
Ganeri, Anita
Season to Season – (Nature's Patterns)
508.2
A full catalogue record for this book is available from the British Library.

Acknowledgements
The Publishers would like to thank the following for permission to reproduce photographs: Corbis pp. **17** (William A Bake), **23** (FLPA), **6** (Graeme Goldin; Cordaiy Photo Library Ltd), **25** (David Keaton), **20** (Bob Krist), **29** (Charles & Josette Lenars), **11** (Douglas Peebles), **13** (Royalty Free), **16** (Ariel Skelley), **10** (Sandro Vannini); NHPA pp. **15** (Laurie Campbell), **21** (Ernie Janes); OFS p. **4**; OFS p. **28** (Dinodia Picture Agency); Photodisc, pp. **5**, **7**, **12**, **14**, **18**, **19**, **22**, **24**, **26**, **27**.

Cover photograph of Crocus in snow is reproduced with permission of Corbis.

Our thanks to David Lewin for his assistance in the preparation of this book.

Every effort has been made to contact copyright holders of any material reproduced in this book. Any omissions will be rectified in subsequent printings if notice is given to the Publishers.

The paper used to print this book comes from sustainable resources.

Contents

Nature's patterns 4

Four seasons 6

Why do we get seasons? 8

Seasons around the world 10

Spring 12

Nature in spring 14

Summer 16

Nature in summer 18

Autumn 20

Nature in autumn 22

Winter 24

Nature in winter 26

Two seasons 28

World seasons map 30

Glossary 31

More books to read 31

Index 32

Words appearing in the text in bold, **like this**, are explained in the Glossary.

Find out more about Nature's Patterns at www.heinemannexplore.co.uk

Nature's patterns

Nature is always changing. Many of the changes that happen follow a **pattern**. This means that they happen over and over again.

Spring is one of the four seasons.

Winter is the coldest season of the year.

The seasons follow a pattern. Some places have four seasons every year. Other places only have two seasons a year.

Four seasons

Many places on Earth have four seasons each year. They are spring, summer, autumn and winter. They happen in the same order each year.

In summer, the weather is usually sunny and warm.

The weather changes as we move from season to season. Which is your favourite season?

In autumn, it starts to get colder. Some trees lose their leaves.

Why do we get seasons?

We get different seasons because the Earth **tilts** to one side as it moves around the Sun. Different parts are tilted towards the Sun at different times of the year.

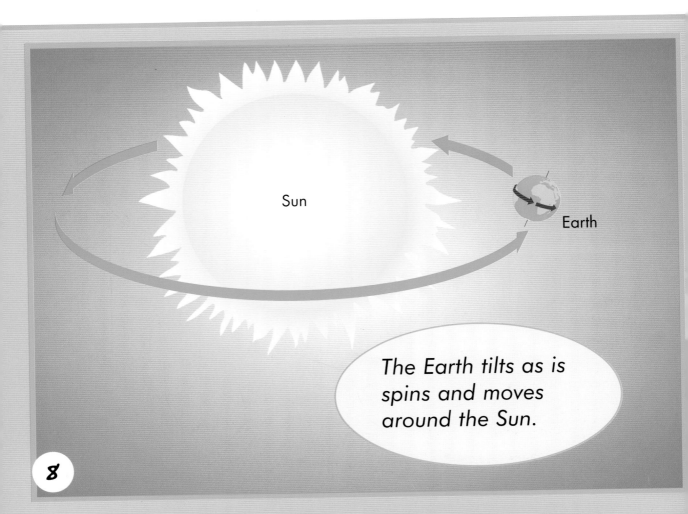

Sun

Earth

The Earth tilts as is spins and moves around the Sun.

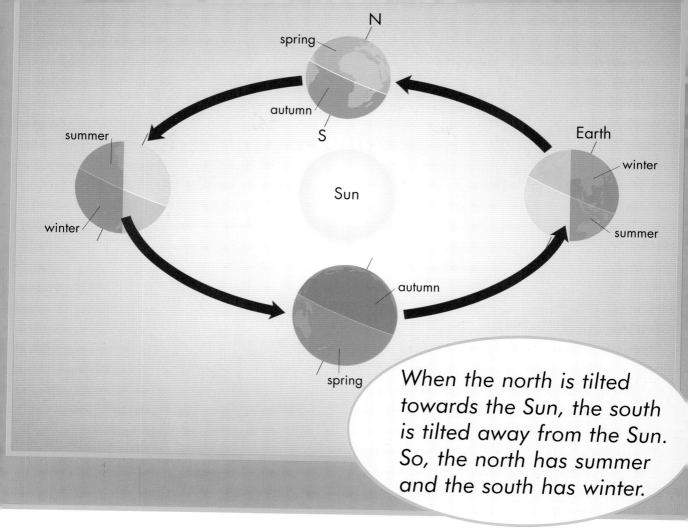

When the north is tilted towards the Sun, the south is tilted away from the Sun. So, the north has summer and the south has winter.

As parts of the Earth are tilted towards the Sun, they get more heat and light. They have spring and summer. As parts are tilted away, they are colder and darker. They have autumn and winter.

9

Seasons around the world

The northern half and the southern half of the Earth have their seasons at different times. Their seasons happen at opposite times of the year.

At Christmas, it is winter in the northern half of the Earth...

When it is summer in the northern half of the Earth, it is winter in the south. When it is winter in the northern half, it is summer in the south.

…but it is summer in the south.

11

Spring

When places on Earth start to be **tilted** towards the Sun, they have spring. The weather gets warmer but there may be some rain.

It often rains in spring.

There is more daylight and the weather is warmer in spring, so plants make flowers.

In spring, places get more sunlight. The days are longer than in winter. It is light for about the same length of time as it is dark.

13

Nature in spring

Spring is the time of year when nature seems to come back to life after the cold of winter. Many baby animals are born in spring.

This calf was born in spring.

The sound of birds singing is a sign that spring is here.

In spring, new leaves and buds start to grow on the trees. Flowers burst into **bloom**. You can also hear birds singing.

Summer

When parts of the Earth are **tilted** towards the Sun the most, they have summer. The Sun shines on the Earth and heats up the ground and the water. It is the warmest time of the year.

It is often warm enough to eat outside in the summer.

In summer, daylight lasts for a long time and darkness for a short time. This means we get long days and short nights.

On a very hot, sticky day there may be a thunderstorm.

Nature in summer

Summer is the time of year when most of nature is in full **bloom**. Trees and plants grow quickly in the warm weather. Farmers' fields are full of **crops**.

Wheat grows quickly in the summer sun.

A holiday by the seaside is fun in the summer.

The summer weather is great for being outdoors. In summer, many people go on holiday to the seaside. The water is warmer so people can swim in the sea.

Autumn

When parts of the Earth start to be **tilted** away from the Sun, they have autumn. The weather starts to get colder but it can still be quite sunny and warm.

In autumn, some days are warm and some days are cold.

In autumn, daylight lasts for a shorter time. Darkness lasts for longer. It begins to get dark quite early in the evening.

Nature in autumn

Autumn is the time of year when nature gets ready for the winter. Many trees start to lose their leaves. First, the leaves change colour.

In autumn, leaves change colour from green to orange and red.

In autumn, farmers **harvest** their **crops**. Animals get ready for winter. Some of them **hibernate** until the weather gets warmer again in spring.

Squirrels store nuts to eat during the winter.

Winter

When parts of the Earth are **tilted** away from the Sun the most, they have winter. It is the coldest time of the year. There can be frost or ice on the ground and it may snow.

Playing in the snow is fun!

In winter, it is dark for much longer than it is light. It is still dark in the morning when you get up. It gets dark early in the evening.

On dark winter evenings, drivers need their lights on so they can see where they are going.

Nature in winter

Winter is the time of year when nature dies down. It is too cold for most plants to grow. Many trees lose their leaves and have bare branches.

Only evergreen plants and trees keep their leaves in winter.

People have to dress in warm clothes to go for a walk in winter.

People have to wrap up warm in the cold weather. But soon spring will come again. Then the **pattern** of the seasons starts all over again.

Two seasons

Some places around the middle of the Earth are near the **equator**. They are never **tilted** away from the Sun. This means that they are always very hot.

The dry season in Africa.

The rainy season in India.

Places near the equator do not have spring, summer, autumn and winter. They have only two seasons, the dry season and the rainy season.

World seasons map

This map shows which parts of the Earth have four seasons and which have only two seasons. Where do you live? How many seasons do you have?

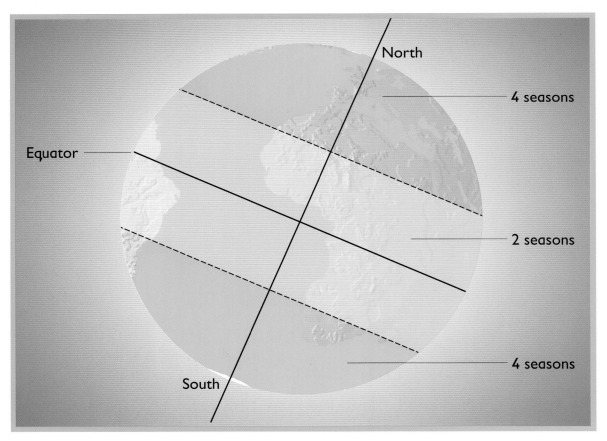

North — 4 seasons

Equator

2 seasons

South — 4 seasons

  Find out more about Nature's Patterns at www.heinemannexplore.co.uk

Glossary

bloom when a plant grows quickly and has flowers

crop plants, such as wheat and barley, that farmers grow in their fields

equator an imaginary line around the middle of the Earth

harvest to cut and bring in crops

hibernate to go into a deep sleep for the winter. Some animals hibernate to stay alive when the weather is cold and there is very little to eat.

pattern something that happens over and over again

tilt to lean to one side

More books to read

Nature's Patterns: Day and Night, Anita Ganeri (Heinemann Library, 2004)

Nature's Patterns: Weather Patterns, Monica Hughes (Heinemann Library, 2004)

Read and Learn: Seasons, Monica Hughes (Raintree, 2004)

Nature's Patterns: Hibernation, Monica Hughes (Heinemann Library, 2004)

Index

autumn 6, 9, 20–23, 29

cold 7, 9, 20, 24, 27

dark 9, 13, 17, 21, 25

day 17, 21

Earth 8–12, 16, 20, 24, 28, 30

light 9, 13, 17, 21, 25

night 17, 25

spring 4–6, 9, 12–15, 23, 27, 29

summer 6, 9, 11, 16–19, 29

Sun 8–9, 12, 16, 20, 24, 28

warm 7, 9, 12, 16–17, 19, 28

weather 7, 12, 18–20, 23, 31

winter 5–6, 9, 11, 13–14, 22–27, 29